History and r...

The Ponts Couverts

I n 1988 Strasbourg celebrated its bimillenium. Indeed, the first mention of the city dates back to 12 B.C. No visible traces of the entrenched Roman camp located at Argentoratum remain today, only the road network is recognizable. The rue des Hallebardes and the rue des Juifs constitute the main east-west axis. As for the north-south axis, it was broken with the building of the cathedral. After the fall of the Roman empire, the town came to life again at the end of the 6th century under the name Strateburg. It was in Strasbourg in 842 that the famous oath

was sworn between Charles the Bald and Ludwig the German, who were allied against their brother Lothaire. It is one of the first documents to have been written in French and German. This period witnessed the beginning of the establishment of the churches. The 13th century was a particularly prosperous period for the town. The agglomeration expanded outside the Roman ramparts and surrounded itself with a ring of walls which has constantly been pushed back over the centuries. The remains of the 13th century walls are still visible in the area of the Ponts Couverts, (the covered bridges),

Rue des Hallebardes : (the «cardo»,
or heart of the Roman camp)

The hospital tower (remains of the 13th century city walls)

the civilian hospital and the Sainte-Madeleine church. The Strasbourg urban fabric is a product of this era in which the churches were already built. Certain recent discoveries in the rue des Juifs and rue des Hallebardes prove that evidence of medieval times can still be unearthed.

The majority of Strasbourg's buildings date from the 16th and 17th centuries. They often consist of a medieval masonned ground floor and several breve floors with half-timbering which are often in a corbelled style. The highly decorated half-timbered houses are one of the characteristics of the city. That of the Maison Kammerzell (Kammerzell house) near the cathedral is indeed remarkable. Other houses, often belonging to patricians, are built

*Place Broglie : the town hall, once the mansion of the counts of Hanau-Lichtenberg (1731-1736)
and the façade of the theatre (1804-1821)*

The Kammerzell house: ground floor 1467, upper floors 1571, angle of the pharmacie du Cerf: ground floor 15th century, upper floors 1567.

in faced. The decoration is concentrated on the front door or the oriel window inherited from the medieval watchtowers. All of these buildings are covered with a steep roof under which the attic is divided into several levels (museum of the Oeuvre Notre-Dame).

The 18th century marked the entrance of the city into the French sphere of influence, following the integration of Strasbourg into the French territory in 1681. Large scale reconstruction work was undertaken, all stamped with the will to break away from "Germanic" tradition. The "Parisian" style private mansion between courtyard and garden was to make its appearance with coated brick walls and freestone emphasizing the corners and openings under a "mansart" style double-pitched roof. The most prestigious examples are those of the palace of the Cardinal de Rohan and the hôtel de Klinglin (hôtel du préfet). The rue Brûlée was to become the street of the private mansions looking onto Place Broglie. This style of architecture was to spread throughout the city, adopting in turn the Regency and Rococo styles, embellished with rocaille motifs or key clasps on the windows on which heads representing the ages of human life, the seasons or the four continents are depicted.

It was the construction work following the bombardments of 1870, destroying amongst other things the great library of Strasbourg in the old Dominican convent which, expanded the town outside the medieval city walls, which had already been pushed back in the 16th century by Specklin. The municipal architect, J. G. Conrath, drew up the project for town planning, much inspired by Hausmann's conception, which used monumental architecture for official buildings, apartment buildings as well

The ponds in the Orangerie park.

Place de la République (late 19th century urban planning)

as private residences. This ensemble included boulevards, inner suburbs, radiating squares, a main east-west axis and a privileged axis linking the imperial residence and the new university. A new axis for traffic was marked out in the old town, the "great gap". Started around 1910 in the rue du 22 Novembre, it was only to be completed around 1960.Due to the difficulties during the inter war period very few impressive buildings were constructed in the first half of the twentieth century. It suffices to mention the Port autonome (1924), the European trade fair (1926), and certain suburbs including Neudorf. In the aftermath of World War II, Strasbourg clung onto its historical past in meticulously restoring damaged buildings such as St. Johns Church and the Rohan Palace. Gradually

The station (1883). The square was given a facelift in 2007 (underground tram station)

Hôtel de Klinglin, steward of Alsace (1730-1736), current Hôtel du Préfet

La Maison de la Radio, Place de Bordeaux (1961), ceramic decoration «The creation of the world» after J. Lurçat

The Esplanade quarter and university buildings (1960-1965). «Pallas Athena», a statue by François Cacheux

L' "Avancée" : offices and housing in the city centre (1997)

«Egyptian» façade, 10 rue du Général Rapp (1905)

Strasbourg began to open up to new ideas in architecture which resulted in several interesting constructions, namely the Palais de la Musique et des Congrès in 1975, the Maison de la radio et de la télévision with its Lurçat mosaic decoration (1968) and the shopping centre Les Halles in 1978. From 1958 onwards, the vast university site was built in the Esplanade residential area with some 55 000 students, including 6 200 from outside France. Since the creation of the Strasbourg Urban community the city has acquired an international dimension in federating the 27 surrounding districts, encompassing over 400 000 inhabitants. More recently some ambitious and impressive architectural projects have been added, namely the Hôtel du Département in 1989, the National School of Administration in 1995 and the Museum of Modern and Contemporary Art (1998).

Since 1949 Strasbourg, with its history-laden past, has been promoted to the rank of a European city. The community institutions- the Council of Europe, the Human Rights Building and the European Parliament- have been installed between the Wacken and the Orangerie. These institutions accentuate the city's radiance which like of New York and Geneva, whilst not being a capital city, houses international organisations.

The Cathedral

Hemmed in by the medieval network of the urban fabric, the cathedral is Strasbourg's symbolic monument. At the end of Rue Mercière, lined with half-timbered 17th century houses, the church dedicated to our Lady was constructed on the highest point of the agglomeration. The western façade, all in pink sandstone, 66 metres high, is a summary of architectural art of the 13th to 15th centuries. Its construction was begun in 1277 under Bishop Conrad of Lichtenberg. The museum of the Oeuvre Notre-Dame possesses a series of plans and projects, including the intention to construct two towers on the façade. Around 1300 the three doorways, as well as their rich sculptured decoration, were finished under the control of Erwin of Steinbach. It was his son who accomplished, around 1340, the great rose window. Under the direction of master Gerlach the square lateral towers were edified between 1340 and 1365. The central space which separates them was the work of Michael of Freiburg in 1384. This level constitutes the platform, from which, after an ascent of 329 steps, we are given a view of the agglomeration and beyond that, the

Vosges and Black Forest. In 1399 the architect of the cathedral of Ulm, Ulrich of Ensingen, undertook the construction of the octagon of the north spire, continued in 1419 and terminated in 1439 by Jean Hültz of Cologne. For more than four centuries, this construction, a true piece of stone lacework rising to 142 metres, was to remain the highest in Western christendom.

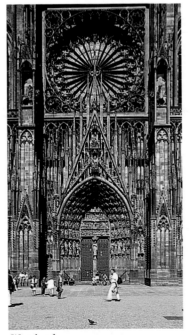

West façade

Constructed during the Gothic period, the Strasbourg cathedral has the distinctive feature of undergoing the same development as the church which preceded it during the Romanesque period. This states well enough the importance of the edifice founded by Bishop Wernher in 1015 which was burnt down several times (as the nave had a wooden ceiling). The building of the present edifice started in 1176 on the east side (the chancel). The lower part of the doorways of the south transept has kept its Roman structure, with its two semi-circular entrances and imposing buttresses. Gothic art, introduced here around 1235 is marked by a change in the decoration of the tympanums and the very conception of the architecture : great lancet bays

The spire

allowing more light to the interior, presence of single-span flying buttresses supporting the thrust of the vaults, and the rose windows which give this architecture the name High Gothic. Between 1772 and 1779 closed stone galleries were built along the sides of the building by Jean Laurent Goetz, which were intended to replace the traders' stalls which had been there since the Middle Ages.

There is a striking contrast between the tower of the transept crossing, the so-called neo-Romanesque Klotz tower (which was renovated in 1997) and the lightness of the Gothic spire of the façade which would have been destroyed during the revolution, had there not been a proposal to cover it with a large metal Phrygian cap.

Transept crossing tower

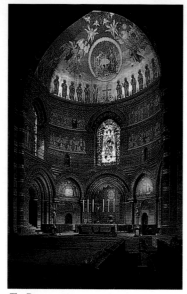

The Roman apse

The "Cantoria"

The eastern part of the cathedral has preserved the Roman structure of the building started in 1176. The chancel is constructed above a sunken crypt. Originally lit by small openings, the semi-circular apse was decorated at the end of the 19th century.

The work on the north transept was in its advanced stages when, around 1235, craftsmen arrived who had been working in the Paris region (maybe at Chartres) and who were familiar with Gothic techniques, already applied to the basilica of Saint-Denis almost one century earlier. The contrast between the imposing volume of the north transept pillar, designed to bear all the weight, and the lightness and thrust of the quatrefoil "Pillar of Angels" on the south side is a prime example of this change in architectural conception. The sculptures on this pillar representing the Last Judgement are also the work of stone masons initiated in the new techniques. Opening into the Saint-André chapel (around 1190), the two semi-circular openings of the transept are flanked by small columns with Romanesque cubic capitals.

Above, almost next to the freestone, there is a nativity scene, which can be linked to the work of Martin Schongauer, around 1500. It is also to a Gothic master that we owe the "cantoria" gallery.

The Pillar of Angels, around 1230-1240

The Mount of Olives (1498) detail

In the nave (34 metres wide and 32 metres high) it is the elevation on three levels (high arches, triforium and clerestory windows) and the supports of the ribbed vaults which convey the best the legibility and balance of 13th century Gothic art structures. Begun in 1240, it was finished in 1275. The lancet windows with their multifoiled forms and the nave contain an exceptional collection of 13th and 14th century glass. The remarkable western rose window completes this collection of great quality.

Some fine pieces of furniture embellish the interior, such as the loft organ in its "swallow's nest" attached to the north wall, dating from 1385. The lower part has survived, decorated with three figures : a herald blowing a trumpet, Samson astride a lion and the bretzel bearer, 'Rohraffe', a statue with movable joints to whom a man hiding in the organ case lent his voice so he could harangue the church goers. The instrument was modified in 1493 and between 1713 and 1716 by André Silbermann.

Finely carved in the late Gothic style, the pulpit was the work of Hans Hammer in 1485. It was put up for the preacher Jean Geyler of Kaisersberg who announced the Reform.

In the north transept, the Mount of Olives (Showing the Roman soldiers going to arrest Christ) comes from the cemetery of Saint-Thomas. Financed in 1498 by Nicolas Roeder, it is attributed to the sculptor Veit Wagner.

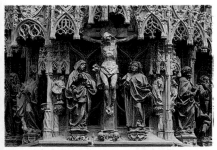

The pulpit, by Hans Hammer, 1485: detail

The organ: gallery, 14th-15th century

The Gothic nave (1240-1275)

Tapestry of the Virgin Mary (mid-17th century)

Detail of the astronomical clock: portrait of Copernicus (1574)

The piece which unquestionably attracts the most curiosity in the cathedral is the astronomical clock and its rotating figurines. It was designe between 1570 and 1574 by the Strasbourg mathematician Dasypodius. The mechanism stopped working in 1780 and was restored between 1838 and 1842 by another Strasbourg genius, Jean Baptiste Schwilgué. Of the original case, decorated by Tobias Stimmer, all the paintwork has been preserved, the most interesting being the portrait of Copernicus which the painters went to copy in Gdansk.

The astronomical clock, designed by Dasypodius (1570-1574), mechanism by Schwilgué (1838-1842)

Reredos in the Saint Laurent chapel

Acquired in 1739 from the church of Notre-Dame de Paris, the wall hanging of the life of the Virgin Mary is composed of 14 tapestries of enormous dimensions (5x5m) which were woven between 1638 and 1657 from cartoons by reputable painters of the time : Philippe de Champaigne, Charles Poerson and Jacques Stella. They bear the arms of Cardinal Richelieu and for the most part originate from the workshops of the Parisian heddle setter Damour. They are only on display in the nave of Strasbourg cathedral during December (the advent period).

After 1681, date of the return of the cathedral to the Catholic religion, 'French' guilds established themselves in Strasbourg. We also owe the altar of the Chapel of St. Laurent to them. This ensemble, a specimen of the art of the Louis XIV period, was delivered in 1698. Strasbourg Cathedral, an outstanding high-Gothic work of art has been, since the Middle Ages, a permanent construction site with striking contrasts of traditional and modern architecture. Although completed at the beginning of the 16th century, it is still under construction, as can be seen from the scaffolding surrounding it and from the workmen who restore this splendid edifice carrying out the same tasks as their stonemason ancestors.

The Cathedral neighborhood

The Kammerzell house and the Cathedral

The cathedral square is surrounded by important residences. At the end of rue Mercière stands the Parmacie du Cerf which has been quoted in documents since 1264. Its 15th century vaulted stone ground floor is topped by two half-timbered floors from the16th (inscribed date 1567) and 17th centuries. The corner pillar supports the corbelled construction of the first floor. Incidentally it is claimed that it was used as a test of the stoutness of the Strasbourg people who had to try and pass behind it without touching it. The

Maison Kammerzell, (Kammerzell house; named after its mid 19th century owner) also possesses a 15th century ground floor (1467) with half-timbered upper floors (here three in number) with a corbelled construction, built after 1587 for a cheese merchant. The half-timbering, pierced by many windows, is richly decorated with wooden sculptures, and the plaster is painted. Since 1879, this residence has been the property of the Oeuvre Notre-Dame. The interior, presently a restaurant, was decorated in the "lansquenet" style by the painter Léo Schnug in 1905.

The Rohan Palace (1732-1742)

Place Kléber, given a facelift in 1994, the Aubette (around 1770)

Détail, 29 rue des Serruriers (1757)

The Rohan Palace, which today houses three museums is a fine example of the architecture imported into Strasbourg during the 18th century. This episcopal palace was built for the Bishop Armand-Gaston de Rohan Soubise, illegitimate son of Louis XIV. The creation of this construction is owed to Joseph Massol, from 1732 to 1742, according to plans drawn up by the king's head architect, Robert de Cotte. Along the Ill, from which it is separated by a terrace, the monumental façade on three levels is punctuated in its centre by Corinthian columns supporting a pediment. At the end of the street is another building completed in 1760 : this is the old Jesuit school, today the Fustel de Coulanges lycée.

Since the construction of tramline A and the work of the architect Clapot in 1994, Place Kléber has become pedestrianised. This open space was conceived in the 18th century by the architect Jean-François Blondel. The Aubette building was his only Strasbourg construction between 1765 and 1778. In the centre stands the statue of General Kléber, inaugurated in 1840. His ashes were placed under the work of the Strasbourg sculptor Philippe Grass. Wandering through the streets, you can discover the intricate decoration of the 18th century faced houses. At 9 rue de l'Epine, the entrance to a mansion constructed by a rich merchant in 1737 is decorated with a rocaille cartouche. The façade of the Poêle des Marchands (the Tradesmens' Stove; meeting place of the guild), 29 rue des Serruriers, dates back to 1757.

Doorway, 9 rue de l'Epine (1737)

Détail, 96 Grand'Rue (1758)

Museum of the Oeuvre Notre-Dame (buildings of 1347 and 1582)

The foundation of the Oeuvre Notre-Dame was created in the mid 13th century and was responsible for the construction and the upkeep of the cathedral. This institution still exists and its former premises at the foot of the cathedral have been occupied since 1931 by a museum containing works of art up until the end of the 17th century. The eastern part of the construction dates back to 1347 and the extension to 1578-1582. This part is the work of T. Uhlberger who installed a beautiful spiral staircase with a helical core in the corner of the old building. The whole is a fine example of medieval and Renaissance Strasbourg architecture and is completed with out-buildings and a small medieval garden. At the end of Pont du Corbeau, formerly known as the Pont des Suppliciés, the history museum, has been housed since 1920 in the former Grande Boucherie (Great slaughter house). Dating back to 1588, this building used to house, on the extremely open ground floor, the butchers' stalls, whilst the first floor and attics served as a market and warehouse. The conception of its open U plan on the Ill has been attributed to Hans Schoch. This neighborhood, until the end of the 19th century, was the business and trade quarter, as is indicated by the riverside building of the Ancienne Douane (Old Customs House) opposite the Grande Boucherie (constructed in 1358 and rebuilt in 1958) where all the merchandise was unloaded.

The Grande Boucherie, 1588 (The history museum)

Chamber of Commerce (1582), place Gutenberg (statue by David d'Angers, 1840)

The former administrative centre of the city of Strasbourg during the Middle Ages, Place Gutenberg now only has one official building left on the west side: this "Neu-Bau" is currently the Chamber of Commerce. Begun in 1582, this building, annexed to the town hall (the medieval Pfalz), was the only monument of the Strasbourg Renaissance to adopt the architectural rules of this period, namely the superposition of the ancient orders level by level. The very steep roofs and the rib vaulted ground floor of medieval tradition have however been preserved. This remarkable construction is attributed to Hans Schoch. The Swiss contractors, Jorg Schmidt and Paul Maurer, left us their signatures in the form of engraved lapidary signs on several freestones. The façade serves as a setting for the statue of Gutenberg, erected in 1840 and is the work of the sculptor David d'Angers. The illustrious printer, who stayed in Strasbourg between 1434 and 1444, is holding a sheet of paper on which is engraved the sibylline motto "and then there was light".

Around the Place du Marché-aux-Cochons-de-Lait, now pedestrianised, stand façades from all periods from the Middle Ages up to the 18th century. On a stone ground floor dating from 1477 and 1602, the corner house boasts three half-timbered upper floors, re-constructed in 1617. This almost entirely intact residence possesses rare open gabled galleries.

At the end of Rue de la Division Leclerc, the most recent development (1930-1936) of the "great gap" begun in 1912, the tram (the work began in 1993) crosses the Saint Nicolas bridge. It passes in front of the "Lauth" house, dating back to 1586. Its gable is embellished with an oriel window, a relic of the medevial watch-tower.

The Saint-Nicolas quai has preserved its quaint "Old Strasbourg" aspect with its faced or half-timbered houses, façades with long cut-off corners or gables dating from the Renaissance up to the 20th century. In the first houses on the quai, which date from the early 17th century, the Alsatian museum is housed. It has preserved its original layout, in particular its interior courtyards and open galleries on the first floor. Traditional apartments have been reconstructed. As for Saint Nicolas' Church, it is the result of several phases of work. The nave dates back to 1381-1387, the choir to 1454, the tower to 1585.

The tram on St Nicolas' bridge and the Lauth house (1586)

The Protestant church of Saint Thomas

The Protestant church of Saint Thomas

The two towers of the Protestant church of Saint Thomas, which dominate the roof tops of Strasbourg, can be easily identified by their shapes: steeply sloping roofs and projecting gables from the medieval period, double-pitched roofs in the French tradition for the Protestant seminary built in 1772 by Samuel Werner, the architect and inspector of city works. Saint Thomas' church, founded in the 6th century, was erected between the 12th and 14th centuries. The high western pillar, completed in 1230, has kept its Romanesque characteristics (such as the arch frieze and pilaster strips) as well as assuming gothic forms (openings in Gothic arches).

In contrast to the exterior, the interior of the church is unique for its soaring Gothic rib vaults, all of the same height. Its construction began in 1260-1270 with the chancel and the transept. The nave dates back to the late 13th century. It was only covered with vaults around 1330, at the same time as the side aisles were being built. There are only a few pieces of stained glass remaining from this period. The furnishings in this edifice are limited at present. The pastoral wooden pulpit dates from the early 19th century. The stone altar was placed next to the Gothic baptismal font in 1744.

The late 13th century nave, vault added in 1330

The tomb of Bishop Adeloch (around 1130)

Saint Thomas's church houses a large number of sepulchral and commemorative monuments of all ages. The mausoleum of the Marshal

Tombstone of Nicolas Roeder (1510)

of Saxony which occupies a section of the chancel wall is uncontestably the most famous of these. It is a major work of 18th century sculpture, donated in 1776-1777 by Jean-Baptiste Pigalle. The conquerer of Fontenoy towers over his vanquished foes : the English leopard, the Dutch lion and the eagle of the Holy Empire. A woman, France, tries in vain to hold him back in his walk to death, whilst a statue of Hercules recalls the military values of the great soldier. The monument, which stands out before a high pyramid, is highlighted by the installation of new windows, the work of Gérard Lardeur in 1985.

The large organ case is all that remains of the organ of Jean-André Silbermann which was installed in 1740 and restored in 1979. The original console of which Mozart "touched the keys in 1778" is preserved in the entrance of the nave.

The mausoleum of the Marshal of Saxony by Pigalle (1777), stained-glass windows by G.Lardeur (1985)

Museums

The Rohan Palace

2 place du Château ———————

The Rohan Palace was built in 1742 (see p. 20-21) and today consists of three museums : the state apartments and decorative arts, the archaeological museum and the museum of Fine Arts.

A glaze realised by Paul Hannong (around 1750), a terrine made up of several recipients (Museum of Decorative Arts)

T he **state apartments**, originally built for Cardinal Armand-Gaston de Rohan Soubise, were restored after the

Multicolour reconstruction of the Koenigshoffen mithraeum (Archaeological museum)

wartime bombing. The main room is the king's chamber, which gives out onto the terrace overlooking the river Ill. Antichambers are on either side of the room, while visitors can also appreciate the synod (dining-room) and the library, with its chapel. All the rooms, including the «small apartments» giving out onto the courtyard, are decorated with furniture from the 18th century.

The Decorative Arts museum is to be found in the west wing of the palace. It is split up into several sections, devoted to furniture, silver and tinware, watchmaking (the astronomical

Antichamber of the Rohan Palace

clock of the cathedral), ceramics, including the faiences of the Hannong family, who ran a highly successful ceramics factory in Strasbourg in the 18th century, with their characteristic blue and multicolour patterns.

The Archaeological Museum, in the palace basement, traces the history of Alsace from prehistoric times up to the year 800. The Gallo-Roman period is well represented, with a number of exhibits originating from digs in the city itself.

The Fine Arts museum, also in the Rohan Palace, features several collections of paintings. The museum dates back to 1898 and visitors can see works of the Flemish schools of the 17th century (Rubens, Van Dyck), as well as paintings by Italian and Spanish artists from the 14th to the 17th centuries, including Giotto, Botticelli, Zurbaran, Veronese, Guardi and Canaletto. France is also well represented, with works by Simon Vouet, Philippe de Champaigne, Le Lorrain, Bouchard and Largillière (16th – 17th centuries).

Canaletto (1697-1768) Venice: View of the Salute, seen from the Grand Canal (Fine Arts Museum).

La Belle Strasbourgeoise, by Nicolas de Largillière, 1703 (Fine Arts Museum).

Museum of the Oeuvre Notre-Dame

3 place du Château ─────

The buildings which used to house the Oeuvre Notre-Dame and the stonecutters' workshop (see p.23) now contain the exhibits of the Museum of the Oeuvre Notre-Dame. An essential part of any visit of the cathedral, visitors can examine original drawings of the cathedral façade and stained-glass windows, as well as a number of statues, near 1500 century pictures from the Upper Rhine (Conrad Witz), works of Sebastien Stoskopf (still-life from the first half of the 17th century), as well as examples of Alsatian furniture.

Statue from the Church and the Synagogue, southern portal of the cathedral transept, around 1230 (Museum of the Oeuvre Notre-Dame).

Near 1200 stained-glass window from the cathedral (Museum of the Oeuvre Notre-Dame).

The Historical Museum

2 rue du Vieux-Marché
aux-Poissons

highly interesting relief-model of Strasbourg, made in 1727, part of the collection made by the military engineers of the school of Vauban for Louis 14th.

The Historical Museum, located within the old Grande Boucherie (Slaughterhouse), a building dating back to 1588 (see p.22-23), is currently being renovated. It traces the history of the city back from the Middle Ages up to the 19th century. The urban topography section features a

Rouget de Lisle singing the Marseillaise, watched by Dietrich, the then mayor of Strasbourg. Painting by Pils (Historical Museum)

The Alsatian Museum

23-25 rue Saint-Nicolas

Alsatian kitchen and a collection of traditional costumes.

The Alsatian Museum is housed within a set of riverside Strasbourg houses dating back to the early 17th century (see p.26). Visitors can see an excellent collection of exhibits showing the everyday life of people in Alsace. The museum also contains a reconstructed chapel, a wine-cellar with its original barrels («loyele») and press, a rustic bedroom, an

«Grosse Stube», reconstruction of the dining area of a communal room in Kochersberg (around 1810) (Alsatian Museum)

The Museum of Modern and Contemporary Art

1 place Jean-Hans Arp ————————

The museum, designed by French architect Adrien Fainsilber (see p. 46), was built in 1998 and contains a remarkable series of sculptures by the Strasbourg-born Jean Arp, as well as significant works by pioneers of abstraction (Kandinsky, Kupka), surrealists (Ernst, Brauner) and other major figures of contemporary art, such as Baselitz and Buren. There is a special section devoted to Gustav Doré.

Sculpture by Jean-Hans Arp "La petite Demeter" (Museum of Modern and Contemporary Art).

Charles Spindler lived in Boersch-Saint-Léonard and produced a series of works influenced by the realist and symbolist movements, as well as art nouveau. (Museum of Modern and Contemporary Art).

Other museums ————————

The Zoological Museum (29 Boulevard de la Victoire) and the Planetarium (4 rue de l'Observatoire) are to be found near the University (see p.55).

The Naviscope, housed within the tug Le Pasteur, moored along the rue du Général Picquart, shows the history of shipping on the Rhine.

he Petite France and the Ponts Couverts

The Ponts Couverts (13th century fortifications, reinforced in the 16th century)

The entrance to the Petite France neigborhood is traditionally marked by the Ponts Couverts (the covered bridges) over the Ill. This part of the town owes its name not to its architecture, but to the presence, in the 16th century, of a hospital where venereal diseases were treated, which was called "zum Französel" (the French disease). The Ponts Couverts are part of the second fortified wall surrounding Strasbourg, which was built between 1200 and 1250 and reinforced throughout the centuries, as attest the 16th century stone spurs which were adapted for firearms. The 13th century brick towers which guard the entrance of the town, were linked up by wooden bridges, and protected by a roof until the 18th century. The present bridges date back to 1860-1870.

Four canals bathe La Petite France. The three that we see here have taken the names of the water mills which they served : Zornmühle, Dinsenmühle and Spitzmühle. The fourth canal was used for navigation. The abundant water supply was also used for the washing of hides in the tanners' district. The main canal is now only used for pleasure boats. Its banks have been developed and the houses which line it, renovated.

The navigation canal

The turn bridge

Place Benjamin Zix

The Place Benjamin Zix is certainly the most attractive part of La Petite France. Developed in 1876-1877 alongside the canal, it was the starting point of the Fossé des Tanneurs ('Tanners' ditch'; on the level of the arched opening in the retaining wall) which was only filled in the 19th century. Most of the houses which line the square and the canal have lofts widely opened up to the outside for they formed drying sheds for the hides. Many of these houses were restored in the 19th century whilst they were still being used for tanning. They almost all have the same structure: above the faced ground floor, two half-timbered corbelled upper floors. The majority of them date back to the 16th and 17th centuries. One of the most well known, "la Maison des Tanneurs" (the Tanners' house) was built in 1572. The hides were hung in the upstairs open galleries, with railings of St Andrew's crosses.

The "Maison des Tanneurs" (1572)

At the foot of recently restored houses, a turning metal bridge has been installed, allowing pedestrians to walk more easily through the area from which cars are excluded.

The lock on the navigation canal

The bank of the Petite France

The passage through the lock of La Petite France is one of the most memorable moments of the cruise around the town. The waters of the four canals meet up at this point. On the left, the restored building (a hotel) housed the old ice suppliers and was the last building to have used hydraulic energy.

Lined with buildings of various colours, the converted banks are an invitation to take a walk all through the year. After Strasbourg came under the French crown in 1681, Vauban decided in 1686 to build, upstream from the Ponts Couverts, a barrage and lock which would make it possible to inundate the waterways of Strasbourg in the event of a siege. This construction was completed in 1700, under the direction of the engineer Tarade. Of the sixteen arches fitted with iron gates, three were raised in 1784 in order to allow the trees uprooted by high waters to pass through more easily. Between 1865 and 1870, as a response to the requirements of modern artillery, the whole construction was lifted onto an arched level in sandstone, brick and earth. It was in 1966 that the decision was taken to open this area to the public and that the panoramic terrace was built.

The Barrage Vauban (1686-1700), raised 1865-1870

The National School of Administration

The Museum of Modern and Contemporary Art by Adrien Fainsilber (1998)

Close by Ponts Couverts a certain number of recently built or restored constructed buildings have added a new spirit to this quarter.

In 1995 the architects Altorffer and Moretti contributed to the restoration of the old prison constructed in 1747, in order to accommodate the National School of Administration and the Centre of European Studies. Very little remains of the old commander's residence of Saint John of Jerusalem, built on this site in 1371 and converted into a hospital in 1520; simply a painted façade facing the road (dating back to 1547) and a few sections of the walls along the Faux Remparts canal which is bordered by one of the towers of the 13th century surrounding wall.

Mixing shapes, colours and materials, the architect Claude Vasconi created the new Hôtel du Département in 1989 in a steadfastly modern and perfectly functional spirit.

On the other side of the river Ill,

the Museum of Modern and Contemporary Art (1994-1998) was designed by Adrien Fainsilber. Opening out on to the waterside, it was built on the site of the former 19th century slaughterhouses.

Hôtel du Département, designed by Vasconi (1989)

The Protestant Church of Saint Pierre-le-Jeune

General view of the cloister

The earliest traces of a place of worship on this site date back to Merovingian times. In 1031 Bishop Guillaume I had a collegiate erected which was consecrated by the Pope Leon IX. All that remains of this building is the late 19th century archaeological reconstruction of the cloister. The present Gothic style church is an edifice for which the work spread from 1290 to 1320, the date of the consecration of the nave by Bishop Jean de Dirpheim.

The long chancel to the east opens into the barely higher nave which is flanked by aisles. The presence of a transept in the west part of the nave is, no doubt, a result of the layout of the 11th century church. The high rib vaults fall on supports without capitals, whereas a large wall surface separates the arcades from the clerestory windows. Other constructions, notably chapels, were added in the 14th and 15th centuries.

The rood-screen and organ

The chancel

The "Navicella" after Giotto

Saint Pierre-le-Jeune is the only building in Strasbourg to have kept its rood-screen in place. This stone gallery which separates the nave from the faithful in the choir and is reserved for the clergy, dates from the early 14th century. The balustrade was installed around 1500. Above the five arcades in gothic arches resting on thin columns the four evangelists are painted. This work, which is in a remarkable state of preservation, was produced by Engelhard in 1620. The vaulted gallery has supported since 1900 the organ of Jean-André Silbermann built in 1780. At the time of its transfer (against the west wall of the nave in the 18th century), it was extended with a postiche façade in the place of the positive organ.

In 1681 Louis XIV returned the chancel to the Catholics, after the whole church had been given over to Protestant worship in 1524. The interior decoration (panelling, statues and paintings) as well as the rocaille style pulpit were replaced around 1765. Above the small neo-Gothic altar, a reredos painted on wood, the work of Wilhelm Stetter (the Lamentation of Christ), recalls the art of Baldung-Grien. Since 1893, the date of the construction of the new Catholic church Saint Pierre-le-Jeune, the whole building is again dedicated to Protestant worship. A large part of the walls of the church is covered by a remarkable collection of 14th century wall paintings. At the time of Schäfer's intervention at the end of the 19th century, certain parts were restored and in other places the scenes were added to (the procession of the nations making its way to the foot of the cross), or even recreated. Without a doubt the most interesting part is the depiction of the "Navicella", St. Peter's boat, against the west well. This is thought to be the oldest known replica of the work of Giotto, which adorned the atrium in St. Peter's church in Rome, a work which has since disappeared. Despite Schäfer's interventions, this painting constitutes one of the major works of pictorial art from the early 14th century.

The bell tower

Avenue de la Liberté

The Préfecture, place de la République

The German "Kaiser" town

The Palais du Rhin, place de la République (1884-1889)

Between the Palais du Rhin, the former imperial residence, and the Palais Universitaire, the old "Kaiser Wilhelm Strasse" constitutes one of the major axes of the new urbanism of the late 19th century. On the east side, lining the Place de la République, two neo-classical style buildings, works of the architects August Hartel and Skjold Neckelmann, face each other. The central reading room of the National University Library is recognizable by the dome which crowns it. Opposite, the former palace of the "Landtag" of Alsace and Lorraine (now the School of Music and National Theatre of Strasbourg). On the north side, the buildings of the former ministeries of Alsace and Lorraine, which today house the Hôtel des Impôts (the tax office) and the Préfecture, built by Ludwig Levy betweeen 1907 and 1911. The Palais du Rhin, the former "Kaiserpalast", closes the square on the north side. The Prussian architect Hermann Eggert took his inspiration from the Italian Renaissance, ancient and baroque, to build, between 1884 and 1889, this edifice, qualified as "elephantesque" by detractors. In the square, in amidst copper beeches and the gingko bilobas stands the Monument to the Dead, sculptered by Drivier and erected in 1936.

Saint Paul's Protestant church (1892)

The School of Decorative Arts (1892)

The Knopf villa house (1905)

The Palais Universitaire (1884) and the statue of Goethe

A bronze statue of Goethe (who was a student in Strasbourg in 1770-1771) graces theatrically the Place de l'Université. This work was by the sculptor Waegener. The university buildings were constructed between 1879 and 1884 by the architect Otto Warth of Karlsruhe.

Beyond the bridge, Saint Paul's neo-Gothic church built by the architect Salomon, between 1889 and 1892, originally intended for Strasbourg's Protestant garrison, rises like a ship's prow at the end of the Ile Sainte-Hélène. In the new residential quarter, the villas all adopt a historicist style. Around 1900, Art Nouveau, here called "Jugendstil", made discreet appearances. The ex Knopf villa in Rue Schiller only borrows a few decorative elements from this style (Berninger and Krafft, 1904-1905). The School of Decorative Arts in rue de l'Académie is the only building which attempted to differentiate itself from the architectural traditions of the end of the century. Based on the plans of Ott (1892), the building is embellished with ceramic motifs from Soufflenheim, after a programme of Anton Seder.

The botanical gardens and the observatory

The Palais de l'Europe and the European Parliament buildings

The Human Rights Building

Strasbourg, European capital

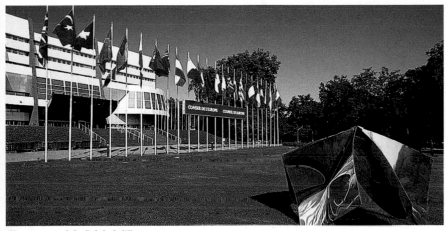

The entrance of the Palais de l'Europe

Situated to the north of Strasbourg, the European quarter has established itself on the confluence of the waters of Ill and the Marne - Rhin canal. The first building to be constructed, the Palais de l'Europe, houses the Council of Europe, an institution created in 1949. The vast building in the shape of a monumental quadrilateral with sloping façades is the work of Henry Bernard and was completed in 1976. The flags of each of the European nations fly high in the square in front of the building. It houses a vast hemicycle in which the meetings of the Council of Europe (43 member states in 2002) take place. Along the canal also tower other European Parliament buildings, designated as IPE (European Parliament Office Blocks). IPE I and II (the offices of the members of parliament) date back to 1980 and are the work of the architect F. Sauer. IPE III was built in 1992.

The architecture of the Human Rights Building (creation of the Commission and Court in 1950) established on the opposite bank of the canal in 1995, contrasts with buildings I and II by its rounded shapes and the long development of the set-back floors. This building, which ressembles a

The Palais Human Rights Building

The Tower of the European Parliament and the Ungemach garden city

Rotunda of the Council of European Union

docked ship, was constructed by Richard Rogers & Partners. It takes on the shape of the waterway (the Ill) which at this point still has its mechanical barrage, installed in 1842.

At the 1992 Edinburgh summit, Strasbourg was chosen as the seat of the European Parliament. This decision led to the construction of a new building to house the 626 Euro MPs, elected by universal suffrage, and the 1000 civil servants. Building IV (the project manager was Architecture Studio Europe) displaying a steadfastly modern architectural style, was completed in 1998. The European Parliament stretches out in the form of a delta alongside the river and a 60 m high tower overlooks the 138 houses located in the Ungemach garden city constructed in 1924-1925.

Located in between the nineteenth century German «Kaiser» town and the Robertsau district, the «European» district brings Strasbourg its status of European capital, this frontier city at a crossroads of cultures and a symbol of reconciliation and cooperation between the peoples of Europe.

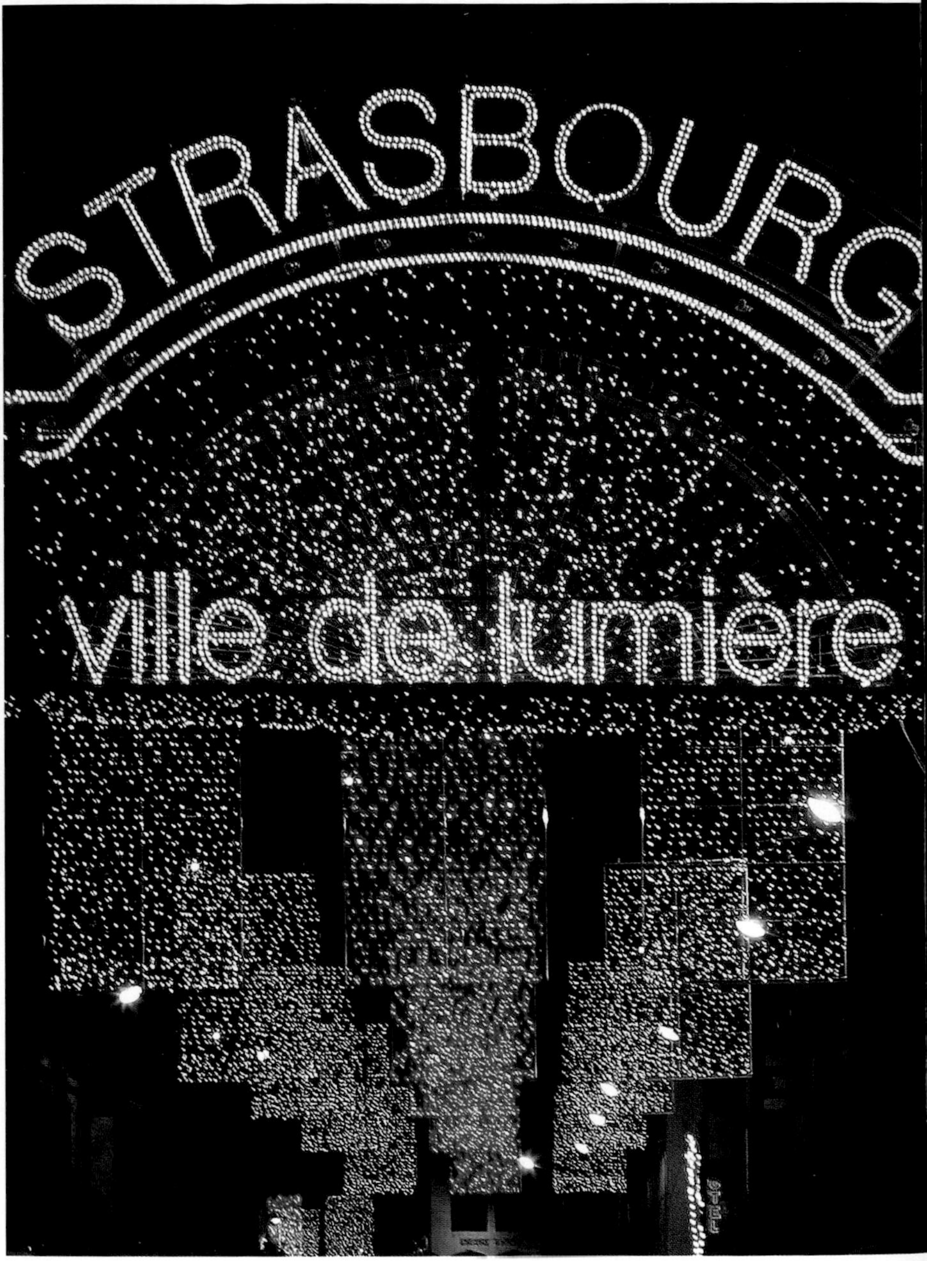
STRASBOURG
ville de lumière

Strasbourg, capital of Christmas

D ecember in Strasbourg means, above all, the immense Christmas market. It was in fact in 1570, under the influence of the Strasbourg Protestants battling against the «extravagant» Catholic traditions, which were so attached to the names of saints, that the Christkindelsmärik (market of the Child Jesus) replaced the market of Saint Nicholas.

Thus the atmosphere which reigns in Strasbourg is unique. It is especially in the late afternoon, just as night is falling, that the magic sets in, as if the city, suddenly conscious of the disappearance of the forces of the sun, compensates for the absence of the heat and light with new ardour : shop windows gleam, decorations twinkle on the facades, the smells of spices and cinnamon bring back childhood memories and Christmas carols drift out from the depths of churches.

The Christmas Market itself spreads out into many streets and squares of the city centre, in particuliar Place Broglie, the Cathedral Square and the Station Square. Several hundreds of stall holders tempt passers-by with original gifts and traditional ornaments for decorating the tree and the nativity scene. There are also many treats to feast on ; sweets, mulled wine, doughnuts... all this from 10 a.m. to 8 p.m.

For good measure, a giant Christmas tree is planted in Place Kleber, there are concerts, giving us a chance to appreciate the beauty of the cathedral and the city's churches, and a whole

host of activities allowing us to discover the rich Alsatian traditions. As for the children, they will love the delightful boat ride through the city.

Our Christmas Legend : who was the Christkindel ?

At the end of the 16th C, the newly reformed church wanted to put an end to the saint Nicholas' day celebrations as they were too pagan. It decided to replace saint Nicholas with the Christkindel, the Christ Child, to remind Man of the sacrifice God had made for him. However the tradition evolved over the centuries and its religious aspect was forgotten.

In the early 19th C, the Christkindel was seen as a veiled young woman dressed in white and wearing a crown of candles on her head; she was bringing presents to children who had been good. Next to her, the fearsome Hans Trapp, one of saint Nicholas' former assistants, continued playing the role of bogeyman. The Christkindel may originally have been a goddess symbolising fertility and announcing the renewal of Nature's annual cycle. On the other hand she may have been Saint Lucie whose day is enthusiastically celebrated in Scandinavian countries.

The booths of the Christmas market, at the foot of the cathedral spire.

FOR ANY INFORMATION, PLEASE CONTACT:
l'Office de Tourisme de Strasbourg et sa Région
17 place de la Cathédrale
67082 STRASBOURG CEDEX
Tél. 03 88 52 28 28 • Fax 03 88 52 28 29
Internet : www.ot-strasbourg.fr- E-mail : info@ot-strasbourg.fr
Bureaux d'accueil
Place de la Cathédrale : Tél. 03 88 52 28 28
Place de la Gare : Tél. 03 88 32 51 49

Dans la même collection **Guide Découverte** :

Le canton de Rosheim : L'habitat (1997) - *Gilbert POINSOT.*

Sur la Route romane : L'église Saint-Pierre et Saint-Paul & le canton de Rosheim (1997) - *Gilbert POINSOT.*

Le canton de Rosheim : Le Patrimoine Religieux (1998) - *Gilbert POINSOT.*

Monastères et Lieux d'Accueil Spirituel Chrétiens d'Alsace (1998) - *Anne HERRIOT, Christophe HAMM*

Le Grand Ried : Patrimoine Naturel (1999) - *Gérard LACOUMETTE.*

CroisiEurope : Chalons - Lyon - Martigues (2000) - *Jean Claude COLIN.*

Terre Romane d'Alsace (2000) - *Gilbert POINSOT.*

La Suisse d'Alsace : Un Paradis Naturel entre vignoble et montagne (2001) - *Jean Claude COLIN.*

Noël en Alsace (2001) - *Jean Claude COLIN.*

Saint-Thomas (2002).

Le Pays de la Zorn (2003) - *Jean Claude COLIN.*

Bouxwiller (2003) - *A. KIEFER.*

Auteur : *Gilbert POINSOT*

Conception : *Studio IMAG'IN*

Photos : *Christophe HAMM*

Photos Inventaire Géneral : *J. Erfurth , C. Menninger, B. Couturier: p. 17 et 23.*
Photos Musées de Strasbourg, p. 32, 39.
Photos Musée d'Art Moderne et Contemporain de Strasbourg, p. 39 - Angèle Plisson

ID L'Edition
9, rue des Artisans - 67210 BERNARDSWILLER
Tél. 03 88 34 22 00 - Fax 03 88 34 26 26 - id.edition@wanadoo.fr
www.id-edition.com
Guide réalisé en collaboration avec l'Office de Tourisme de Strasbourg

N° ISBN 2-9511273-8-3
2éme trimestre 2011

Marzolff's statue of the Rhine fisherman (1908) on the J.F. Kennedy bridge. The spires of the Protestant ➤
church of St. Paul (1892) and the cathedral (finished in 1439) can be seen in the background.